FINDING THE SPIRIT

Written and
Illustrated by

VANESSA
CASTRO

Contents

Chapter 1 The Fall ....Page 5

Chapter 2 Loneliness ....Page 11

Chapter 3 Introducing Disabilities ....Page 17

Chapter 4 In Denial ....Page 27

Chapter 5 The Potluck Games ....Page 35

Chapter 6 Will Justin Ever Get Over His
Stubbornness? ....Page 45

Chapter 7 A Breakthrough ....Page 55

Chapter 8 Exploding Vs. Accessibility ....Page 65

Chapter 9 Preparation ....Page 73

Chapter 10 Game One ....Page 77

Chapter 11 Game Two ....Page 83

Chapter 12 The Final Game ....Page 87

Conclusion ....Page 95

Chapter 1
The Fall

After school, Saratina and Justin raced home together where their babysitter, Laurie, prepared them a snack. Then the two kids ran outside to the backyard and climbed up the ladder to their treehouse. That was their favorite place to hang out, and they could stay there for hours.

One particularly stormy day, after Saratina and Justin finished their snack, they raced up the treehouse without realizing how wet and slippery the steps were.

Justin climbed up as fast as he could but slipped and fell on his back. He screamed, "Ouch!!! I can't move my legs. Help me!" "Oh stop kidding around. Get up." Saratina said. Justin cried out, "I'm not kidding around! I can't get up! Help me!"

Saratina ran into the house, leaving track marks on the floor with her wet shoes yelling, "Laurie! Laurie! Where are you?" Laurie answered, "I'm watching TV. What is it?" Running into the family room, Saratina screamed, "Help! Justin fell and can't get up!" "Oh my goodness! Where is he?" Laurie responded as she removed the blanket from her lap and jumped off the couch.

Saratina grabbed Laurie's hand and they ran outside. Laurie kneeled down on the ground beside him and asked, "Justin what's wrong, Hun? What happened?"

"He fell," Saratina answered.

"I can't move my legs," cried Justin. As Laurie tried to help him get up, he screamed, "Ouch! My back... it hurts!"

"Saratina, go get my cell phone," instructed Laurie with a concerned look on her face. She asked Justin if he was sure that he could not move his legs. Justin told her that he could not feel anything from the waist down.

"Oh my goodness!," cried Laurie, wondering if Justin was seriously injured. She grabbed the cellphone from Saratina and dialed 9-1-1. In the blink of an eye the ambulance arrived. As Justin was already in pain and frightened, they told him that he needed to go the hospital.

The ambulance was ready to leave when Justin's parents, Mr. and Mrs. Anderson, drove up. They got out of their car and looked confused, wondering what was happening. Laurie quickly explained and they all rushed to the hospital.

As soon as they arrived, they took x-rays of Justin's back and lower body and immediately performed surgery on him. After a few hours in the operating room, Dr. Lapham came out and gave the news to Justin's parents. "When Justin fell on his back, he injured his spinal cord, fracturing two of his lower lumbar vertebrae. We've done all that we could to get the bones to heal properly, but it looks like Justin is now a paraplegic."

"A para what?" asked the parents. Dr. Lapham explained, "Someone who is a paraplegic is unable to use the lower half of their body. It is an impairment in motor and sensory function of the lower extremities caused by Justin's spinal cord injury. The lower part of his body is now paralyzed. The good news is that he is still able to use the upper part of his body like his arms and hands. However, Justin will probably never be able to walk again."

"Never walk again?!" Justin's mother, Maria, cried. "What do you mean?"

"Maybe with intense physical therapy or perhaps in a few years the bone will be strong enough to bear weight." Dr. Lapham continued, "but if or when that will happen is uncertain. I'm afraid that It looks like Justin will need a wheelchair."

"What? Me in a wheelchair? No!" yelled Justin and began to cry. Justin's mother put her arms around him and asked the doctor, "Are you sure about this?"

Dr. Lapham responded, "I'm sorry Mrs. Derson. I know this is very difficult for all of you. Like I said I did all that I could. You're welcome to get a second opinion, but I'm sure that any other doctor would tell you the same thing."

"But he's only eleven years old!" Justin's mother cried.

Justin then realized, "My soccer game! My soccer game is Saturday! I have to be there!"

"I'm sorry kiddo," said Dr. Lapham "You can go, but I'm afraid you won't be able to play."

Justin sat in the hospital bed feeling miserable with tears in his eyes.

Chapter 2
Loneliness

Saturday morning came and Justin was feeling very lonely. He knew that all of his friends were at the soccer game. He thought that no one would ever want to hang out with him again, because now he was disabled and in a wheelchair.

Two months had gone by and Justin's soccer team made it to the championship game. Unfortunately, Justin lost his spirits and isolated himself in his room watching TV and playing video games all day.

"Why don't you go to the soccer game today?" Justin's mother suggested. "It'll be good for you to go outside and see your friends."

"Why should I go see them? None of them have bothered to come see me."

"That's not true Justin. Saratina, Jeff, Peter, and Erik have come by, but you refuse to see anybody." Justin rolled his eyes as his mom continued, "I know this is really difficult for you Sweetie, but you can't isolate yourself from the world."

"Why not?" cried Justin as he lifted up the bottom of his shirt to wipe his eyes. "Who wants to hang around someone in a wheelchair?"

As his mom got up from his bed and brought him a box of tissue she said, "Well I guess Peter, Jeff and Erik do. And Saratina has been over almost every day just to see how you are doing."

"They're just being nice," he said in an annoyed way. "Can you go? The A's game is on soon."

Justin's mom left the room, shut the door and wondered what to do. How could she make him feel better? "My poor baby," she said as she sat down on the living room floor and began to cry.

Later that afternoon there was an unexpected knock on the door. It was Justin's entire soccer team screaming, celebrating, and yelling, "WE WON! WE WON!! We are the champions!"

"Where's Justin? He should celebrate with us," said Erik. "He's in his room, but I don't think you'll get much enthusiasm from him. You can try," Justin's mom said.

While Erik and the team went to Justin's room, Coach Steve asked Justin's mother how he was doing.

She told him how he had been isolating himself and refusing to do anything.

"After school he comes straight home and locks himself in his room. Do you have any suggestions of what to do? I'd love to hear them."

Coach Steve told her that he heard what's been happening with Justin from the other kids and that's why he brought the team over. He hoped that the team would be able to cheer Justin up. Maria was very appreciative of Steve's thoughtfulness. He also suggested that Justin should be a part of a team and play soccer again.

"How?" Justin's mother asked very confused. "He can no longer walk."

"Well, there are ways. For instance, Justin could be a part of another soccer team. I have a friend who teaches power soccer."

"What's power soccer?" Maria asks.

Steve told Maria, "It's wheelchair soccer. Some describe it as bumper car with wheelchairs and a ball. Instead of kicking the ball with their feet, they hit the ball with bumper guards that are attached to their wheelchairs. It might be helpful for Justin to interact with other kids who are also in wheelchairs. From what my friend tells me, those kids have a blast."

"That sounds fun," said Maria.

Steve continued, "In the United States power soccer was the first competitive team sport designed and developed specifically for athletes with disabilities such as quadriplegia, paraplegia, multiple sclerosis, muscular dystrophy, cerebral palsy, and many others who use power wheelchairs."

"Geez. I never knew there are so many types of disabilities," Maria replied. "Do you think Justin will like that? He has never been around anyone with a disability."

Steve replied, "It's worth a shot. My friend, Tatianna, coaches a power soccer team at the school. She's great with kids with disabilities, and has been working with them for years. She's also very athletic. She swims, rollerblades, plays tennis, and coaches power soccer. I bet if anyone can cheer Justin up and get him active again, Tatianna will be the one. She's super friendly and very energetic. You should bring Justin to the school's gymnasium on Wednesday afternoon. You guys can meet her and watch her power soccer team practice."

With much consideration, Maria agreed to talk to Justin about going to meet her.

Chapter 3
Introducing Disabilities

Three weeks later, Justin agreed to go meet Tatianna. Maria pushed Justin into the gymnasium, and there were several kids in wheelchairs rolling around, laughing, screaming, and hitting balls all over the place.

Tatianna spotted them by the door and rolled over and said, "Hello, I'm Tatianna. You must be Justin and Maria." She stuck out her hand for Justin. Justin shook her hand and said hello.

Tatianna had long beautiful red hair in a ponytail. She was wearing a purple and white striped referee dress and had matching purple rollerblades on. Tatianna said Steve told her about Justin and hoped that Justin will eventually join the team. Maria asked Tatianna if all of the kids were in wheelchairs because of accidents.

Tatianna answered, "No. Not all of them. Some of them were born with disabilities like

Cerebral Palsy, Spina Bifida, Muscular Dystrophy, Autism, Quadriplegic, etc... Some have a combination of disabilities. For example, Bianca, is deaf and has Cerebral Palsy."

"WOW! How does that happen?" Maria was curious. Tatianna shrugged her shoulders and said, "That's one of the many mysteries of life." "How do you talk to Bianca if she's deaf?" Justin asked Tatianna. With her fingers, Tatiana said "By using sign language."

"I thought I am here to play soccer, not to talk with my hands," Justin said in an irritated voice.

"Of course you're here to play soccer. I'm just letting you know that we accommodate all disabilities on this soccer team. Besides teaching power soccer, I try to teach my students to accept each other for who they are regardless of what limitations they have. The only rules I have for my team is that everyone has to respect each other. Some may not like each other, but they must find ways to get along and communicate with one another. We have to work together as a powerful team!" Tatianna said enthusiastically, throwing both fists up in the air. Maria was amazed that there were so many disabilities that she never heard of.

"I want to go home," Justin told his mom.

"Home? Why?" asked Maria.

"I don't belong here. All of these people are in wheelchairs." Tatianna smiled and told him that everyone on the team was very friendly and he should give it a chance. "I promise you will enjoy yourself."

Maria said to Justin, "I know this is very difficult for you, Hon. Between your accident and no longer being able to walk, I can only imagine how you feel. If I could do anything to make you walk again, believe me I would. But I can't. I don't know what to do to make you feel better. All I know is that you can't continue hiding in your room, just watching TV and playing video games all day."

Tatianna suggested, "Justin, why don't you try joining the power soccer team for a month, and if you don't like it, you can stop coming." Maria and Justin thought that was a good idea, and he agreed to let Tatianna introduce him to the team called The Hot Wheels.

Tatianna pushed him over to the group and introduced everyone. Then she told Justin that they needed to put him in a power chair since the game was called power soccer. So she rolled him to the wall where they had extra power chairs. She asked Justin if he had tried driving a power chair.

He answered, "No,"

"Oh, you're going to love it. You won't have to depend on your mom or anyone else to push you around. Which chair do you want to try?" Justin pointed to the black one closest to him. Tatianna picked him up and put him in the power chair, buckled the seatbelt, and said, "you definitely need to have your seatbelt on for safety. This team gets wild, and the last thing I need is to have you slip out of your chair."

"Have any of your students fallen out of their chairs?" Maria asked concern. "Only once when I first started. A student's seatbelt wasn't on, and she crashed into another student and slid right out of her chair. Scared the crap out of me. From then on I always make sure that everybody has their seat belts. Safety first," Tatianna told them.

"Was the student hurt?" Maria asked. "No. She was fine. She was laughing her head off," answered Tatianna laughing. "Oh, the memories."

Then she put the bumper guard around the footrest. She explained, "You hit the ball with the bumper guard. It also protects your legs and feet from getting hurt."

Tatianna said laughing, "Speaking of protecting feet from getting hurt, I wear rollerblades every time we practice. These power chairs are heavy and when someone runs over my feet, it's very painful. Believe me, I've had my feet ran over many times so I finally learned my lesson and got rollerblades. It's not as easy for power chairs to run over my feet now. Plus, it's a lot easier to roll around in these instead of wearing tennis shoes, running around, and trying to keep up with all these kids in power chairs."

Once the bumper guards were safely secured, Tatianna showed him the joystick and explained, "To turn it on you hit this switch. To go forward, you push the joystick forward. To go backwards, you push the joystick backwards. Left is left and right is right."

"It's like playing video games," Justin replied as he started driving. He crashed into some of the other chairs, the walls, and almost hit his mom and Tatianna in the legs. "This is fun!"

Maria nervously Tatianna if she could slow down the speed, concerned that he might hurt himself or someone else.

"We could, but that's the same speed as all of the other chairs, which is five miles per hour. If he wants to play power soccer, he needs to learn how to drive and control the chair at that speed."

"WOW! Five miles per hour! Isn't that

too fast and dangerous?" Maria was very nervous. "Like I said, that's the average speed for all of these chairs. When we play against other power soccer teams, their chairs need to be at the same speed to make it fair for all of the players." Tatianna explained. "This is more fun than playing video games!" Justin yelled.

After a few minutes of letting Justin practice driving the chair, Tatianna went over some basic rules about the sport. "The ball can only be played by the player's power chair. If the ball touches any other part of the player's body, it's a foul. In other words, you can only use your power chair to hit the ball. You cannot use your hands.

"Just like regular soccer," Justin told her. "Exactly. Also, you may noticed that the balls we use in power soccer are smaller than regular soccer balls." Tatianna grabbed a ball and said, "the circumference of a regular soccer ball is 23-24 inches and weighs 11-12 ounces. The size of a power soccer ball is usually 33cm (13 inches). This size is an appropriate pressure so it minimizes bouncing and prevents power chairs from riding over it.

"What happens if someone runs over the ball and pops it?" Justin asked. "If the ball bursts or becomes defective during a play, then we have to restart that play. And to make goals, you hit the ball between those two orange poles at the end of each side of the gym. The goal areas are 8 m (26 ft 3 inches) wide and 5m (16 ft 5 inches) deep." Tatianna explained as she pointed to the poles. "Do you understand?"

Justin nodded yes.

Tatianna also explained, "During a match both teams can only have four players on the field at a time that includes one goalkeeper per team."

"Only four players? That means only eight of us can play at a time. It looks like there's a lot more than eight people in this gym right now. On Steve's soccer team, we had eleven players per team on the field. Why can only four members be on the field during a play? That doesn't make sense."

Tatianna said, "Since all of the member on this team have disabilities, we have to accommodate to each person and their specific needs and abilities. There are members who are on ventilators. Others have respiratory problems, and others just get tired easy due to their disabilities. It all depends on the individual, so I make sure that each member gets to play on the field for at least ten minutes."

Maria was stunned, "With respiratory problems and kids on ventilators, how are they able to play at all? I assume power soccer is a very energetic game."

"It is," Tatianna continued. "All of the members on this team love power soccer. Plus, it allows them to be athletic, competitive, and be a part of a team. It also gives them a chance to socialize with others who have similar disabilities. For some of the members, coming to practice and being on this team makes them feel like this is the only place where they really belong."

"Really? Why is that?" Maria is very curious. "Because most people here in Adelina County just don't know how to treat others with disabilities, including some of their family members," answered Tatianna.

"WOW! We are definitely learning a lot today. Aren't we Justin?" Maria said.

Justin was confused and asked, "How can the members only play for ten minutes? That doesn't make sense. In regular soccer, I was out on the field playing for about 45 minutes."

Tatianna said, "Yeah, but that's regular soccer. This is power soccer, and in power soccer the games are only 40 minutes. Two 20 minute periods"

"What? 40 minutes? Only 40 minutes? Regular soccer games are 90 minutes long. Why are power soccer games so short? That's not even half the game of regular soccer" Justin asked very confused.

"That's the game," replied Tatianna. "Yeah, but we spend more time just sitting around than actually playing. That sucks," said Justin.

"Well, in regular soccer you only played for half of the game and for the rest of the time you sat on the sidelines and watched, right?" Tatianna asked.

"Yeah, but it was 45 minutes of playing. Not just 10 minutes."

"I know but power soccer games are adapted for disabled athletes, so we have to adapt to everybody's capabilities," Tatianna explained.

Justin was getting bored and asked in an aggravating tone, "Are we going to play power soccer today or what?"

"Okay, you're right." Tatianna blew her whistle and yelled, "Let's get back to playing soccer! Are you ready, Justin?"

Justin yelled out, "Yes, I am and it's about time!"

Chapter 4
In Denial

Even though Justin had hesitations about being on the team, he continued going to practice and shortly became a pro at driving the power chair. After a few weeks, Tatianna noticed that Justin wasn't socializing with any of his new teammates. She pulled him aside and said, "Hey Justin. Have you talked to any of the team members yet?"

Justin replied, "No."

Tatianna asked, "Why not? Everyone is very friendly."

"They're all in wheelchairs and disabled." Tatianna replied, "Yeah, so are you." Justin rolled his eyes. "Look, I know that you are still getting used to being in a chair and trying to accept that, but you need to let your family and friends support you. That's why Steve and your mom thought it would be good for you to join this team. So you could interact with friends who have some idea of what you are going through."

"Have any of them fallen from a tree and can no longer walk?" asked Justin.

Tatianna answered, "No, but they aren't able to walk. So we thought having you be around others who are in wheelchairs and love playing soccer like you do would help you start adjusting to your new situation."

Justin felt annoyed and started driving away. However, Tatianna was so used to running after power chairs, especially with her rollerblades on, that she grabbed onto the handles on the back of his wheelchair. He realized she was rolling away with him when her long red hair flew in his face.

Tatianna said, "Sorry Dude, but you can't get away from me that easily."

Justin suddenly stopped and asked, "What do you want from me?"

She told him to become more of a team player and talk to the other members once in awhile. She pointed out, "The other members of the team have been nice. They've taught you how to play power soccer and how to hit the ball with the chair. But you haven't thanked anyone. When you come at the beginning of practice you don't say even hello to anyone. What's up with that?"

Justin shrugged his shoulders.

Tatianna asked, "If you're shy, it's okay. Or are you uncomfortable being here? Whatever it is, let me know so I can help you." Justin didn't know how to answer her. Tatianna told him, "If you can't be a team player, I'm afraid that I'm going have to cut you from the team."

He didn't say anything else to her for the rest of the day.

During dinner that evening Justin's dad asked him how soccer practice was. Without any expression Justin said, "Fine."

"Just fine?" Justin's dad asked. "Last week you were telling us about speeding around the gym, crashing into the other members trying to make a goal. No stories like that today?"

Justin shook his head and continued eating his dinner. "You seem awfully quiet tonight. Is everything alright?" asked his mom.

"No! Tatianna says I have to start talking to the other members on the team. If I don't, then I can't play soccer."

"Well, don't you already talk to them?" His dad asked. Justin shook his head, "No. Why should I? They're all in wheelchairs."

"I see," said Justin's dad. "So you don't like the group?"

"They're all in wheelchairs."

"That doesn't answer the question. If you

don't like the group then maybe you should stop going," suggested his dad as he chewed his pork chops.

"If he quits the team, what's he going to do? Lock himself in his room all day again?" asked his mom. Then she looked at Justin, "Is there any other reason why you don't talk to the team other than the fact that they are in wheelchairs?"

Justin said, "No."

"Well Hon, maybe you should imagine your teammates aren't in wheelchairs. You can look at their smiling faces instead, specially when they make those goals."

Justin looked at her like she was nuts. "How do I imagine them not in wheelchairs?" His mom said, "We're all sitting in chairs right now eating dinner, right?"

Justin nodded yes.

"When you look at our faces, do you see the chairs that we're sitting in?" Justin answered, "Yeah, when I look down."

"You're not supposed to look down, Kiddo. Your mom wants you to look at our faces," his dad replied.

"Okay, and then what?" Justin replied in an annoyed voice.

"When you think about us, or any of your friends like Saratina or Erik, do you think

about the chairs that we sit in?" asked his
mom.

"No."

"Well, that's what you need to start doing
with the members of your new soccer team."

"What?"

"You need to look at their faces and start
talking to them. Get to know them, and then
maybe you will forget about their wheelchairs."

Justin looked at her like she was nuts and
said, "I'm done eating. Can I go to my room?"
"Sure," his mom replied, not knowing what
else to say.

The next day Maria called Tatianna to
recap what Justin told her. Tatianna said,
"Even though Justin enjoys playing soccer, he
needs to start interacting and socializing with
the other team members. Once he starts doing
that, I know that he will enjoy being on this
team more. His confidence will build, and
hopefully, he will realize it's not so bad being
in a wheelchair. I know what happened is dev-
astating and that he will probably never walk
again, but I think eventually this will make
him stronger."

"Do you have any ideas on how to get him
to start talking to the other kids?" Maria wondered.

"Well, how was he on the other team?" Maria answered, "He was fine. He was a normal eleven year old boy who loved playing soccer and had a lot of friends. He used to hang out with them, or they would come over.

Justin never had any trouble making friends and interacting with others. I guess this accident really did a number on him-both physically and emotionally."

"It sounds like it definitely did, which is understandable," Tatianna replied. "Don't worry. A light bulb just came on in my head, and I have an idea."

"Okay. What is it?" Maria was curious. "We can have a big potluck for both of the soccer teams here at the school. They can meet, pig out on hot dogs, hamburgers, chips, dip, etc... and they can talk about soccer, video games, school, or whatever. I think if Justin see his old teammates talking to his new teammates who are in wheelchairs, he will be less intimidated by them."

"What makes you think Justin's friends will talk to the disabled kids?"

Tatianna replied, "Oh, I've been working with kids for over fifteen years and usually kids will talk to anybody. Plus, this will be a fun social event here at school. I will also talk to Steve and tell him my idea, and have him talk to his team as well. This will be fun."

"Okay, keep me posted," replied Maria.

Chapter 5
The Potluck Games

A month later Tatianna and Steve planned a potluck in the schoolyard for the two soccer teams and their families. There was food and games.

Tatiana and Steve made spaces at the tables so several students in wheelchairs could sit with the non-disabled students as well as their families.

While everyone was socializing, Maria noticed that several of Justin's friends began talking and laughing with some of the students in wheelchairs.

In the meantime, Justin was hanging out with his buds, Erik and Saratina. Maria suggested that they talk to some of the disabled students.

Saratina took a bite of her burger and said, "I said hi to Leslie earlier. She's cool. She definitely enjoys playing power soccer."

"Cool," Maria said. "What about you, Justin? Have you gotten to know anyone on your new soccer team yet?"

"Nope," he replied with food in his mouth. Erik said, "I talked to Brian and helped him get his burger."

"Oh, that's nice. What did you talk about?" asked Maria.

"Brian likes watching baseball. The A's are his favorite team," Erik replied.

"WOW! The A's. Isn't that you favorite team, Sweetie?" Maria asked Justin. Justin answered, "Yes," and continued eating.

"Maybe after you finish eating, you and Erik can talk about the A's with Brian," Maria suggested.Erik said, "Okay." But Justin just rolled his eyes and was more interested in the food.

Tatiana blew her whistle and yelled out into a megaphone. "It's game time!!!!!!!!!!!" Everyone looked up, eager to hear what the game was.

Tatiana yelled, "We need half of my team in front of me and the other half in front of Steve." Justin rolled over to Steve's side.

"Now we need half of Steve's team on my side and half on Steve's side." While the kids were running to the sides that they wanted to be on, Tatianna began to explain the game.

"Divide into groups of four. Each group must have two wheelchairs and two able bodies."

Justin teamed up with Erik, Saratina, and Brian."Are you all in groups of four?" Tatianna asked through the megaphone.

"Yes!!!!!!!!!!!!!" they shouted out."This game is a relay race. You have to run or roll through the obstacle course holding a soccer ball. Each of your team members will be waiting for the ball to be handed to them by every orange cone. If you drop the ball while you're running, you have to go back to the orange cone and start running. When you hand the ball to your team member in a wheelchair, make sure that they get the ball. You might have to physically move their hands on the ball to make sure they've got a good hold. If the ball falls or rolls off their lap, they will also have to go back to the orange cone and start over. The team that crosses the finish line wins. Does everyone understand?"

"YES!!!!" the crowd shouted out. Tatiana continued, "Okay, decide who's first, second, third, and forth, and get into positions. On your mark, get set, go!"

Parents, family members, and others were cheering them on as the children ran through the obstacle course, soccer balls flying everywhere. Thirty-five minutes later, Tatianna announced, "The winners are Melissa, Josh, Kenny, and Louis! Yay! Good job you guys!"

The next game required two people in power chairs to talk to each other and create an art project using objects on tables. As Tatianna picked up each item she explained, "You have paints, construction paper, glue, different colors of string, clay, styrofoam, etc. Since most of our disabled students aren't able to use their hands very well, the non- disabled students will be their hands. The first ten minutes of this challenge, the two students in the wheelchairs on each team must talk and decide together what they are going to create and how they are going to do it. In in meantime, the non-disabled students will be hanging out right here by the stage, so they can't hear their groups. Does everyone understand?"

Everyone yelled out, "Yes!"

"Okay, I need all the non-disabled kids over here by the stage now please. Everyone in chairs head over to the picnic tables by those trees. Remember, two to a table."

While the kids were going to the tables, Tatianna purposely walked over to the table with Justin to observe him interacting with Brian. She asked, "What are you guys going to create?"

Brian looked at Justin and asked what he thought. Justin said, "An alien." Brian said, "Cool. What should it look like?"

Instead of answering Brian, Justin started cutting some construction paper and began designing an alien by himself.

Tatianna reminded Justin, "This is a team project. You need to explain to Brian what you are doing and then you guys will need to work together to tell your other team members how to create the alien because they will be blindfolded."

"Blindfolded? You didn't say anything about them being blindfolded," Brian laughed.

"I know. I like to keep you guys guessing," Tatianna laughed.

Brian looked at Justin and said, "So you need to talk to me and tell me what you are trying to create."

Justin looked at Tatianna and asked, "Why do I need to tell Brian what I'm doing? Why can't I just tell Erik and Saratina?"

She answered, "Because that's the rules of the game. You need to communicate and work with all of your team members. If you don't want to be a team player, you might as well go home." Justin didn't know what to say. Tatianna continued, "Time is ticking away, so I suggest you guys start talking to each other and figure out how to tell your other teammates how to create this alien." Brian said, "Dude, talk to me. What are you doing with this rolled up construction paper and all these other things?"

Justin felt annoyed, knowing that Tatianna wouldn't go away until he said something to Brian. Justin took a deep breath and started abruptly telling Brian his ideas.

"This big styrofoam ball can be the head. We can roll up construction paper for the body. These pipe cleaners can be antennas popping out of his head."

He continued,"We can roll up construction paper for the body. These pipe cleaners can be antennas popping out of his head."

"Good job. See, that wasn't so hard." Tatianna told him.

Suddenly, a whistle went off and Steve yelled through the megaphone "Times up! Now we need to blindfold these kids." Once they were blindfolded, they were taken to their groups.

Erik and Saratina were taken to Justin and Brian's table. Tatianna told the boys to explain what they were making to Erik and Saratina.

"We are making an alien," said Justin

"How are we supposed to do that with these blindfolds?" Erik laughed.

Tatianna told the group that with Justin and Brian guiding them, handing them the materials and talking to each other, they would have an awesome alien.

Saratina laughed, "Okay. What do we do?" Brian held up a big styrofoam ball for Saratina and Erik to feel, and told them that was the head. Then Justin had no problem telling Saratina and Erik to roll up the construction paper for the body and glue the styrofoam ball to it.

Tatianna listened and wondered how to make Justin feel that comfortable talking to all of the kids.

Brian yelled out, "Hurry up! Time is running

out!"

Erik laughed, "You try doing this blindfolded."
Steve blew his whistle and yelled through the
megaphone, "Time's up! Stop what you are doing.

The three judges will go around each table and
look at your creations. They are judging on three
things: 1. The creativity of the use of the materials, 2. How well your group communicated with
each other, and 3. How well your project came out.
If your group was successful in all three, you could
win."

Brian said, "We lost."

Erik asked, "Why?"

"Because Justin wouldn't tell me his ideas. Tatianna had to make him talk to me."

"That's unusual for Justin." Erik responded
surprisingly and turned to Justin and asked, "How
come you won't talk to Brian? He's cool."

Justin said, "I did."

Brian responded, "Barely, after Tatianna told
him to."

Erik looked at Justin and asked, "Why?"

"Because he's in a wheelchair," Justin replied.

"Yeah, and so are you," said Erik.

Justin just shook his head.

The three judges walked over to their table, in-
specting their alien. They enjoyed seeing the
children's creativity and asked how well the group
worked together.

Erik and Saratina told them they communicated just fine while being blindfolded, but Brian informed them that it was difficult for him to work with Justin, and he explained why. The judges didn't like the lack of communication among the group, so they could not make them the winners.

Brian turns to Erik and said, "I told you." Once again Erik asked Justin why was it so difficult for him to speak to Brian. Brian looked at Justin and said, "See Dude, you cost us the game."

At this point, Justin was upset and drove his wheelchair to his mom. "I want to go home," he told her. Maria was confused, and Justin would not tell her what happened. He just kept insisting that they leave, so they left.

Chapter 6
Will Justin Ever Get Over His Stubbornness?

The following week, Tatianna called a meeting with Justin and his mother. She was frustrated with Justin and asked him how he would feel if no one spoke to him just because he was in a wheelchair.

"Well, if no one on the power soccer team talks to me that will be fine." Justin answered shrugging his shoulders.

"No, I don't mean anyone who is disabled. I'm talking about all of your old buddies like Erik, Jeff, Peter, Saratina, me, Steve, etc... What would you do if all of us decided not to talk to you ever again just because you're in a wheelchair? How would you feel?" Tatianna asked.

"They've been talking to me after my accident, so why would they stop?"

"Well, you never know. You might do or say something that makes them mad and they could stop talking to you. And then what?"

Justin said, "They didn't talk to me when I had my accident."

His mom reminded him, "You know that is not true. They tried visiting but you didn't want to see anyone."

Tatianna interjected, "Correct me if I'm wrong, but didn't he start getting out of his funk and getting back to his old self when he joined my power soccer team?"

Maria said, "Oh yeah. That's right." Then she looked at Justin and said, "See, without realizing it Tatianna's team helped you get out of your room and out of your depression."

"How?" Justin was curious.

Maria explained to him, "Once you joined the new team, you started looking forward to going to practice. You started coming home with stories from practice. And you reached out to your old friends again."

Tatianna said, "Like it or not, I think this team is good for you. I think you should at least try talking to them." Justin rolled his eyes. Tatianna continued, "If you want people to be kind and friendly to you despite your disability, you have to start treating others the same."

"She's right," Maria said. "Remember I told you that once you get to know your team members you would probably forget that they are in wheelchairs?"

"If he doesn't start talking to the other team members then I'm afraid that I'll have to kick

Justin off the team," Tatianna firmly told them.

That night Maria asked Justin how he felt about what Tatianna said. He wasn't sure how to respond. "Do you really want to get kicked off the team?"

"I want to play soccer," he replied.
"Well, you will need to start speaking to your team members otherwise no soccer," Maria firmly told him.

For weeks Justin didn't go to practice. He just went to school and came home and played video games. None of his friends came to visit him. Then one day Tatianna popped up at his door.

Justin was surprised and asked what she was doing at his house.

Tatianna said, "You thought I gave up on you, huh? Well, I didn't. I've worked with students too long to give up."

Justin was confused and didn't know what she meant.

Tatianna said, "I'm going to help you overcome your fear of talking to people with disabilities. Once I commit to something I do it, and right now I am committed to helping you."

Justin looked at her confused and not sure what to say.

Tatianna told him she was planing a lunch for him and some of his teammates who she thought Justin would get along with after he could get over his stubbornness.

"Like who?" he asked.

"I'm thinking Brain, Tom, Mike, and Kevin. Maybe a couple more. What do you think about those guys?"

Justin shrugged his shoulders and said, "I don't know. What are we going to do at the lunch?"

"Well, besides eating lunch you guys can talk."

"Talk about what?"

" Soccer or other sports or anything you want, my friend. I just need you to socialize with others and realize that having a disability isn't as bad as it seems."

Justin asked, "When will this lunch be?"

Tatianna said, "The day after tomorrow at the pizzeria across the street from school. Don't be late."

She began walking out of the house and Justin said, "Wait. Is anyone else coming? Like any of my friends who are not disabled?"

"Besides me? Nope. Just us. It'll be fun!" Tatianna continued walking out.

The day of the lunch, Justin told his mom that he didn't want to go. She told him, "Sometimes we all have to do things that we don't want to do because they can be beneficial."

"How can having lunch with guys in wheelchairs be beneficial?"

Maria rolled her eyes. She was starting to feel

annoyed at having the same conversation. "You're going to this lunch, and I hope you and the guys will talk, eat, and laugh."

Justin rolled his eyes and said, "Okay." Maria walked him into the pizzeria. "I love you Hon. Have fun," she said as she walked away.

Tatianna and the guys welcomed Justin as he rolled up to the table. Tatianna poured him a glass of lemonade and asked the guys what kind of pizza they wanted. "While I go order, you guys talk among yourselves."

Brian asked Justin, "So Dude, who is your favorite soccer player?"

"David Beckham," he responded without looking at him.

"Yes, David Beckham is awesome!" Brian replied and all of the other guys agreed.

"I wish I could kick the ball as hard as David Beckham can," Mike said.

"I used to," Justin said.

"You used to what?" Mike asked.

"Kick the ball as hard as David Beckham," Justin replied.

Mike laughed and said, "Come on, dude. No one kicks the ball like David Beckham. That's why he won so many games and won the world cup twice."

"You didn't know me before my accident, so how do you know I couldn't kick as hard as David

Beckham?"

"I'm just saying that not everyone can kick like him."

Tatianna returned to the table with the pizzas, "How's it going guys?"

Brian answered, "Well, we found out that Justin's favorite soccer player is David Beckham." "Yes! You guys got him to talk to you. That's what I like to hear!" Tatianna said enthusiastically.

"Yeah, but Mike doesn't believe me that I could kick the ball as hard as David Beckham," said Justin.

Mike said, "Dude, I never said I didn't believe you. I just said no one kicks like him."

Tatianna replied positively, "I'm sure Justin was able to kick the ball pretty hard. You can't be on a soccer team without having strong legs, right?"

"Unless, they are on our team," responded Tom with a mouth full of pizza. "For our team, we just need a powerful chair to get the balls in the goals."

"Yep. That's right," Mike agreed. "For our soccer team, the chairs just need to be fully charged. That's all that matters."

"Well, that isn't all that matters. You should also like the game and have team spirit. After all, soccer is a team sport," said Tatianna.

"So how do you like the team Justin? Are you

ready to talk to us yet?" asked Mike.

"What do you mean? I've been talking to you guys since I got here."

"Yeah, and you've been with the team for months and this is the first I heard you say more than two words," Mike told him.

Justin just rolled his eyes. Tatianna said, "Let's relax. Remember Justin joined the team after a major accident, so it's natural that he would need time to adjust to his new normal. We all just need to be patient and help him in any way we can. We are a team." She turned to Justin, "I'm proud that you are finally starting to talk to these guys. Believe me, the more you are around the team, the easier it will be."

"The easier what will be?" asked Justin.

"Talking to us," Brian said to him.

Tatianna explained to Justin, "The more you talk to your friends on this team, the more you'll realize that it's just like hanging out with your other friends. The only difference is this group is always sitting down. Right guys?"

Everyone nodded and agreed. Tatianna continued, "Then hopefully, you will build confidence in your new self."

After lunch Maria picked Justin up and asked how it went. Tatianna said he made a little break through, and he and the guys were talking about David Beckham. "I'm proud of him."

"That's great. He loves David Beckham," replied Maria.

"Yeah. Who doesn't love David Beckham? He's hot." Tatianna laughed and continued, "Slowly but surely Justin is coming around. We just have to keep working on him."

Maria thanked her and follwed Justin as he rolled out.

Chapter 7
A Breakthrough

That night after Justin went to bed, David Beckham and Tatianna were in his dream. They told him that in spite of his limitations with using a wheelchair, he could do anything that he puts his mind to. Although his soccer team members were all in wheelchairs, he could show others that The Hot Wheels were a unique, awesome and ,owerful team.

David Beckham and Tatianna also told him that with his knowledge and love for soccer, he could help the sport of power soccer be well known in his community. Tatianna told Justin, "Anything is possible if you put your mind to it. Learning how to accept yourself and facing the challenges you have are all part of life. You can mope, groan, be lonely, and feel sorry for yourself, but that's no fun. Or you can take the positive things that people give you and help others with situations similar to yours. Unfortunately, people have freak accidents every so often, but I believe that there is a reason for everything. You just have to find it within yourself. I have a feeling that you will be able to show others that even though you became a paraplegic, you have the ability to overcome obstacles and still live an active life with the love and support of your friends and family. So get out of your funk, find your inner strength, and enjoy life. Let yourself be the David Beckham of power soccer."

That sentence, "Let yourself be the David Beckham of power soccer," struck a chord with Justin.

The following morning Justin woke up with a new perspective on life. He could not wait to get to soccer practice. His mom was happy yet very confused by the sudden change in his attitude. Justin told her that Tatianna and David Beckham told him that he could do anything.

"What? David Beckham? What are you talking about?" She asked very confused.

"At practice today I will teach the team how to really play soccer, just how I played when I was on my old team."

"Huh, how are you going to do that? Remember you're in a wheelchair now."

"Yes, I know but I'm going to do it!" Justin was very enthusiastic.

"Do you realize this means you actually have to speak to your other teammates who are in wheelchairs?" Maria asked.

"Yep. I know."

"Who are you and where is my son?" Maria asked in a surprised voice.

That afternoon at practice, Justin actually said hello to everybody. It was a quite a surprise for Tatianna and the team. Then he started taking charge by putting his hands to his mouth and announcing to the team, "Okay you guys, we need to get our act together and become the best power team ever!!!"

Everyone looked around asking, "What's going on?"

"What? Justin speaks?" one girl said to another. "I guess so," another girl responded shrugging her shoulders. "I've never heard him say a word." "Yeah, neither have I. I thought he had a speech impediment," said the first girl.

Tatianna asked Justin, "What's going on? What are you doing?"

Justin told her and the team confidently, "I'm taking the Hot Wheels to the championships." Everybody looked so confused and didn't know what to say.

Mike rudely said to him, "You barely said anything to any of us since you've been on the team, and suddenly, you want to take us to a championships."

"Yes, I want to take us to the championships," Mike replied in disbelief, "First of all, that makes no sense. Secondly, why should we listen to you? You don't even like being on this team because we are in wheelchairs. And thirdly, what the heck do you know about power soccer? You've been on the team for a few months."

Justin explained to Mike and the rest of them about his dream with Tatianna and David Beckham and that they told him that he can help take this team to the championships. They all thought he was joking around. Everyone started to laugh.

"I never knew you were a comedian," Brian said. "Erik and Saratina said you were funny, but I had a hard time believing it until now." Then he turned to face the team and jokingly said, "I guess we're going to the championships! Yay!"

"I'm serious! Watch me!" Justin confidently told them.

Tatianna told him that she was extremely ecstatic and proud that he was finally communicating with the team. However, she definitely didn't expect him to take charge and take the team to the championships.

"Have the Hot Wheels ever won a championship title?" Justin asked her.

"No, not yet." Tatianna answered, taken back by Justin's brand new attitude and motivation.

"Well, what are we waiting for? Let's go to the championships." Justin told her enthusiastically.

Still confused, Tatianna asked, "Wait. What

exactly did I say in your dream which made you completely change your attitude?"

"You and David Beckham said I could do anything if I put my mind to it. Even though, I am now a paraplegic and have some limitations, I should use my love of soccer to help make others aware of power soccer."

"WOW!" Tatianna laughed, "I've been told that I've made an impact in my students' lives several times, but I've never been told I was in a dream with David Beckham. I knew there was a reason why I like him... Did we also tell you to take our team to the championships in your dream?"

"You guys said to use my love for soccer to make others aware of power soccer. I missed being in the championships with my old team because of my accident, which was very unfair. So one way or another, I will be in a championship soccer game," Justin firmly said.

"I love your new attitude and determination. I know with everyone's determination, knowledge, hard work, and love for power soccer, this team could definitely win a championship." Tatianna replied encouragingly.

The team was still very confused and weary about Justin's new attitude. Mike asked, "Why is Justin now in charge? He hasn't said a single word to any of us since he joined the team. I should be in charge. I've been here for five years."

Then he turned to Justin and said, "Why don't you give us some examples to prove that you know something about power soccer."

Justin said, "Okay, I think Tyrone is the best goalkeeper on the team because he blocks the ball better than Tom or Melissa."

"Why do you think that?" Tom asked. "Because you let too many balls slip past you." Justin answered.

"I liked you better when you weren't talking." Tom told him rolling his eyes.

"Yeah, me too," said Melissa.

"I'm just being honest," replied Justin.

"Okay Mr. Smarty Pants, who do you think scores the most goals and who are the best defenders on our team?" Mike asked. "Well, Brian, Greg, and I make the most goals," answered Justin.

"Yeah, you would include yourself," Mike said in a snarky voice.

Justin continued, "For the best defense, that would be Mario, Tenika, Chris, and Bruce."

Tatianna said, "Yeah, I'd say Justin's observations are pretty accurate. However, I would include Sofia, Stefanie, and Jack as good defenders. Alex, Mike, and you, Justin, are also good at scoring goals."

Mike told Justin, "See, according to Tatianna I'm a great player."

"I never said you weren't," Justin replied back. Then Mike turned to the rest of the team and said, "Just because you guys might agree with Justin's observations, I still don't think he should be in charge."

Tatianna said, "Calm down. I'm still in charge, and I never said that Justin was in charge. But those who want to help take the team to the championships can be co-leaders. I would love that. Team work!"

Mike said, "Well, since I've been here the longest, I should definitely do it. But I still don't think Justin is qualified to be a co-leader."

"Why not?" Justin asked loudly. "I already told you why. You don't like any of us," Mike shouted back.

"Okay, if you don't want to go to the championships that's your problem." replied Justin.

That made Mike angry and he drove his wheelchair right into the side of Justin's wheelchair. It made a loud crash. Luckily nothing broke.

Tatianna blew her whistle and yelled, "That's enough! Mike, go sit on the sideline now!", as she went to make sure that Justin was alright.

"But I still think he barely knows anything about power soccer! Plus, he hasn't denied that he doesn't like any of us," Mike yelled.

"Maybe not, but right now his attitude is better than yours, so go." Tatianna said in a stern voice pointing to the sideline. Mike drove off to the side.

Tatianna turned back to the group and said, "If we want to get to the championships, we better start practicing."

Everyone was pumped up and excited. "Whoo-woo! Let's do it!"

Tatianna turned to Justin, "So Justin, since this was your idea, what's your strategy for us to get to the top?"

"To make lots of goals and win win win! We should have Tyrone be the main goalkeeper so other teams can't score as easily."

"Sounds good to me," Tatianna said enthusiastically blowing her whistle. "Everyone, get into position and let's get started!"

Chapter 8
Exploding Vs.
Accessibility

After a few months of practicing with the group, Justin finally seemed comfortable being around others with disabilities. His confidence built back up, and he realized how much he enjoyed power soccer. At home, he began watching videos on his computer, gathering any information about power soccer that he could. He began bringing his laptop to show videos and the latest updates to practice, sharing them so that the entire team could improve. This really helped the team get stronger on their offense and defense, leading to them scoring more goals.

There were only a few power soccer teams in Adelina County, and the Hot Wheels competed against them at the end of each school year. One day, Justin told Tatianna that he thought they should start playing outside their county. Tatianna was curious, "You do? And why do you want to play outside the county?"

"So the Hot Wheels can get more practice and publicity. The more teams we play, the closer we get to winning the championship."

"I love your enthusiasm! It's such a one eighty from when I first met you." Tatianna told him with a huge grin.

"Well, doesn't that make sense?" Justin asked while spinning a soccer ball on his lap.

"I'll need to talk to Principal Randoff and see if we can arrange some power soccer games outside Adelina County. Don't be surprised if she turns us down. It's not easy transporting twenty-five students in power wheelchairs. Plus, all of the equipment and staff. It will definitely be a challenge," Tatianna told the team.

Justin suggested that they all talk to Principal Randoff together. "Just like you always tell us, we have to work together as a team."

Tatianna looked at Justin and said, "Who are you? What happened to the shy, quiet, stubborn eleven year boy who I met a year ago? What did I do to you? Or was it David Beckham?"

Justin shrugged his shoulders and said, "I don't know."

"Well, whatever happened I love it! Should I ask Principal Randoff to come here one day so we can talk to her?"

All together the team shouted, "YES!"
"Alright, I'll see what I can do," said Tatianna.

A week later, Principal Randoff came to practice. After she thanked the group for inviting her, she told them that she was very interested to hear that they wanted to go play other teams outside their county and onto the championships. However, it would be impossible to do due to several things.

"Well, what are they?" Mike said, "I've been on this team for five years. It's about time we try going for the championships. Right you guys?"

Everyone said, "Yes!"

Principal Randoff told them, "I love the energy and the enthusiasm from this team. It's great! However, we don't have the funding." Then she asked Tatianna how many members were on the team, and she answered twenty five. Principal Randoff continued telling the team, "There are twenty five of you, so we would need at least five or six wheelchair accessible buses, which is definitely not in our budget. I'm sorry but it's just not possible."

"What about public transportation?" asked one student.

"Taking public transportation within our county is one thing because it's only two or three trips towards the end of the year. However, if you guys go to other counties throughout the school year that would be too much planning and organizing."

Justin said to her, "Tatianna said I could do anything if I put my mind to it. And so did David Beckham"

Principal Randoff was confused. "Who's David Beckham?"

"One of the most famous soccer players in the world," he replied.

"Oh, I didn't know you knew him," Principal Randoff said.

"I don't. At least not yet, but one day after I win the power soccer championship, he will want to know me," Justin told her very confidently.

Still a bit confused, Principal Randoff told the team, "I'm proud that you all have confidence in wanting and believing that you can go all the way to the championships. Unfortunately, we just don't have the funding. Sorry."

Seeing how bummed the team was, Tatianna said, "Although, we might not be able to go the championships this year, we still can become the champions of our county of Adelina." They didn't quite understand what she meant by this. Tatianna explained that they could make the county games into their own championships. "We can't go straight to the top right away. We have to work towards our goals. If your goal is to win the championships of all of the power soccer teams, you have to work for it, which means starting locally."

Mike said, "We've been playing the local teams since I've been here and that was five years ago. It's about time for this team to explode."

"Yeah, I totally hear what you're saying, Mike. But we can't just jump on the bus and go. You also need to remember that everyone on this team has different limitations due to all of the unique disabilities, so it wouldn't be as easy to jump up and go as it would be if we were a regular soccer team." Tatianna said.

"But I've been practicing for years. I'm ready to become a champion," Mike told her in an aggravated tone.

"Do you know that David Beckham had to practice for years before winning the World Cup twice? That's what we need to do. Practice and work together."

Justin said to Mike, "It was my idea to go to the championships. Not yours."

Tatianna rolled her eyes and told them, "It doesn't matter who's idea it was. We are not discussing this again." Then she turned to the team, "What I want to know is if you guys want to make our county games into our championship games?" The team answered, "Yes!"

"But how would that work?" asked Justin. Tatianna replied, "If the Hot Wheels win the first two local games, making it to the final game, I will find a way to get it televised. Then after the game, there could be a ceremony." Everyone became very excited. Tatianna continued, "If I get the final game on TV it will definitely raise awareness of power soccer and you guys will be famous!"

Every member on the Hot Wheels became very excited. Justin said, "Wouldn't it be cool if David Beckham saw us on TV and decided to come meet us?"

Tatianna said, "You never know. We might meet him one day. Anything is possible."

The possibility of meeting David Beckham motivated the team even more. "What are we waiting for? Let's start practicing!" yelled Justin.

Chapter 9
Preparation

It was three months until their first game, so they started practicing two hours a day, five days a week. On the days when Tatianna couldn't make it to practice, Justin took charge and created new strategies for them to score more goals. Tatianna was amazed how dedicated he was. She jokingly said, "Geez, soon you guys won't need me anymore since Justin is taking over my job."

The three months zoomed by quickly. Before they knew it, the first game was two weeks away. Everyone could feel the excitement as they did their last minute training. Tatianna worked tirelessly to get them ready for the big games, gathering all of the equipment and figuring out the transportation for all twenty five of the team members who were all in power wheelchairs. This required lots of planning, so she set up a meeting with all of the parents for help. Fortunately, ten of her students had wheelchair accessible vans. However, only a few of them could fit two wheelchairs. Not realizing how difficult it was to transport a group of students in wheelchairs from point A to point B, this meeting was an eye opener for Maria. "WOW! We just can't get a regular school bus."

Tatianna said, "I wish it was that easy but no. Most regular school buses are not wheelchair accessible. That's why we need to coordinate. We do this every year."

"I see," Maria said. "Do the parents do most of the driving?"

"It depends on whether or not they have a wheelchair accessible van and how many wheelchairs it fits."

Maria asked, "Since there aren't enough parents with vans, what are we going to do?"
Justin jokingly said, "I know. We can just tie all of the equipment on the back of all of our wheelchairs and roll there."

"The game is thirty-nine miles away on the other end of Adelina County. How would I and the other staff get there if you all roll?" Tatianna laughed.

"You all can put on some rollerblades and just hold on to a wheelchair," Justin replied laughing.

"You've got quite an imagination. But I highly doubt that Principal Randoff would allow twenty-five students in wheelchairs and the staff in rollerblades to cruise across the freeway and on the streets to the other end of the county." Tatianna said laughing. "Although, it would save us money."

"Oh come on. That would be fun!" Justin laughed.

"Yes, fun but dangerous. I'll need to talk to Principal Randoff. I'll let you all know what we come up with."

Two days later, with the ten parents driving their own vans, Principal Randoff agreed to rent two big wheelchair accessible vans that would fit the rest of the team and staff.

Chapter 10
Game One

With the transportation in place, the Hot Wheels were ready to go beat the opposing team, The Rolling Dragons. The morning of the first big game, they met at the school's parking lot and off they went.

Once they arrived at the gymnasium, The Rolling Dragons were already there warming up. Family and friends kept coming in, filling up the bleachers.

The team started getting ready, putting on their red jerseys that said "Hot Wheels" and their numbers on the front. Tatianna went around asking "Is everyone's seat belt and bumper guard secured? Great! Are you guys ready to rock and roll?" Even though some kids were nervous they were all very excited to get the game started.

As the first half rolled on, it was obvious that the Hot Wheels nerves took over. They were unable to follow through with their plays and get the ball in the goal.

Unfortunately, by halftime the Hot Wheels had not scored a single point. The Rolling Dragons were leading by two points.

The Hot Wheels were feeling down, so Tatianna gave them a pep talk. "Even though, we're behind two points right now, we still have 20 minutes to play, I know you can do it! You guys are the Hot Wheels! Just think of everything we practiced and all of the techniques we did to score."

"Should I be the goalkeeper for the next five minutes?" Tyrone asked.

Tatianna responded, "Yes, That's a good idea. Also, let's move Stefanie, Mario, and Bruce to offense. Let's have Brian and Chris as offenders. Justin and Mike will be midfielders. Is everyone cool with that?"

The team shouted out, "YES!"

Tatianna continued, "Okay, you guys just need to focus and at the same time relax. Enjoy yourselves and all of the nerves will disappear. Think of David Beckham. Imagine how many games he must have played before winning his first championship game. If by any chance we don't win this game, there will be many more. I am extremely proud of each and every one of you for all of the extra hours of practice you put in. Now go back out there and score those goals!!! I know you guys can do it!"

That pep talk pumped the team up. They went back on the field and Stefanie quickly scored their first goal. The Hot Wheels were so relieved and happy. Shortly after, Mario scored their second goal, making the score even with the Rolling Dragons. Two to two. There was only one minute and thirteen seconds left in the game. Suddenly, Justin got a hold of the ball and hit it as hard as he could with his wheelchair and it flew straight into the goal, giving The Hot Wheels the winning point!

Principal Randoff grabbed a microphone and announced, "The winners of this power soccer game, with a score of 3 to 2, are The Hot Wheels!"

As the crowd cheered wildly, Justin's team members kept hugging him and giving him high fives. Realizing that he just scored the winning goal Justin was ecstatic! As Brian patted him on the back, Justin exclaimed, "I never imagined that after my accident I would play soccer ever again, let alone lead my team to victory." This was definitely the best day Justin had since his accident.

Tatianna excitedly announced, "The Hot

Wheels will be going to another big power soccer game in Adelina County in two weeks!" The cheers and excitement continued for hours.

Chapter 11
Game Two

The next two weeks were full of practice and discussing their mistakes and what they needed to do differently. Transportation was already in place, so the morning of game two they were ready to go.

Their second game was at another school in Adelina County against The Viking Rockets. When they arrived, tons of people were already there. The Hot Wheels' energy was pumped up knowing that if they won this game they would be going to the championships.

Within the first five minutes of the game Brian scored the first goal for the Hot Wheels. Shortly after, The Vikings Rockets made a goal, and then another point ten minutes later. By halftime The Hot Wheels were behind by two points again.

This time Justin gave his teammates the pep talk. "Come on guys. We can do it! We were in a similar position last time, and we can beat them. So let's do it again!"

Now that The Hot Wheels were reenergized, they got back out on the field. "Let's get ready to kick butt!" yelled Justin.

They scored three more points, making them in the lead by one point. With one minute remaining, The Vikings Rockets scored another goal, so after twenty minutes of playing the score was tied up four to four.

They had to go to overtime.

With a minute and twenty seconds to go, each team huddled up to plan their final strategies.

Tatianna continued encouraging her team, yelling, "You guys got this! You only need one more goal and it's off to the championships!"

The team cheered as they got ready to win the game.

The clock was down to twenty-two seconds when Mike scored the final goal. The Hot Wheels won with the final score of five to four.

They were heading to the championship game! Everyone on the team exploded with joy and excitement. Justin yelled, "Our team is on a hot winning streak!"

Chapter 12
The Final Game

When they arrived at the Calistoga Arena on the morning of the game, Tatianna gathered her team,"This is the biggest arena in Adelina County!" She continued, "I know you guys have been working hard. Since we couldn't afford to leave Adelina County to go win the real power soccer championship of the country, I thought this would be the next best thing."

"I didn't realize the Calistoga Arena is so huge! Now we've got to be the Power Tigers!" exclaimed Mike.

The team's eyes were wide open seeing that

the arena filled with all of the people who came to watch the game. The local TV crew from VCSH was setting up their cameras and equipment. A newscaster put a microphone in Tatianna's face saying, "A wheelchair event has never before been televised in Adelina County before. A lot of people in this county had been minimally exposed to people in wheelchairs. Do you consider this to be a unique event?"

Tatianna replied, "Yes I do! I've always wanted to spread awareness about disabilities and the sport of power soccer. With this awesome team, I knew it would be the perfect opportunity to do it!"

Justin felt like he was about to play in the World Cup. "Is this how David Beckham feels before a championship game?" He thought to himself.

Justin looked up into the bleachers and saw all his friends from his old soccer team like Saratina, Erik, Jeff, Peter, and Laurie, as well as his former babysitter. "They all came to support us and cheer us on!" Justin thought. They came over and started congratulating him on getting to this big game, wishing him luck, hugging, and giving him high fives.

Justin's former coach, Steve, went up to him and said, "I've been keeping up with you and your progress through Tatianna, and I'm just so unbe-

-lievably proud of you! You were one of my best soccer students, but I never imagined after your accident you would be such a force to be reckoned with. You are an amazing dude! Good luck today!" He bent over and gave Justin a hug.

"Thanks! We're going to beat the Power Tigers!" Justin replied very confidently.

"We'll be rooting for you," Steve replied.
At the beginning of the game, the choir clubs of both schools' teams got together and sang the National Anthem in front of the audience.

Shortly after that the teams rolled out onto the field as each name was announced. The crowd's cheering added even more energy and excitement.

When the Power Tigers scored the first goal within the first three minutes, the crowd went wild.

Justin put his hands up to his mouth and told his team, "It's okay, there is still lots of time. Just block the ball!" Shortly after, The Hot Wheels scored their first goal, followed by another one. Tatianna was on the sidelines jumping up and down screaming at top of her lungs cheering her team on. "YES! Come on! You guys got this!"

Right before half time Justin made a goal, putting his team in the lead three to one.

During halftime both teams huddled up. Tatianna told her team, "Even though we are in the lead, we can't take it for granted. You guys need to continue playing as if they are right behind, just like the previous two games."

Justin told the team, "Come on guys! We are twenty minutes away from being the first power soccer champions of Adelina County! Let's do this!"

Mike said, "I've waited five years to be in a championship game. There's no way I'm rolling out of here without that trophy."

"Don't you mean we?" Justin asked.

Mike said, "Yeah, sure. We. Us. Whatever. Let's just win this game!"

Justin just shook his head and let it go, and said, "Let's do this!"

Tatianna gave them instructions on what they could do to prevent the Power Tigers from scoring. "For the next five minutes, Tenika, stay on number 34 since she scored the first goal. And the rest of you, just keep blocking. When you see an opening to score, you know what to do."

"Yes! We do!" Shouted the team.

It was time for the second half to begin, and as the players headed back onto the field, the crowd was going wild, yelling and cheering.

Unfortunately, The Power Tigers caught up, making the score tied three to three.

Justin and the Hot Wheels started getting nervous, but they heard Tatianna say, "Don't worry. Just do what we practiced." Their friends and family were cheering them on. "Come on! You guys got this! Let's go Hot Wheels! Let's go!"

The energy of the crowd got the Hot Wheels pumped up and with four minutes left to play, Justin scored another point. The crowd went wild. A minute later the Power Tigers retaliated with another point.

With thirty-eight seconds left in the game Justin got a hold of the ball and hit it as hard as he could. The ball flew right into the goal. Justin had scored the winning point!

Astonished, he threw his arms up and ran in circles around the field to hug his teammates.

The whole arena went ballistic with cheers and excitement.

An announcer took a mic and said, "Ladies and Gentlemen. I'm happy to announce that with the final score of five to four, the very first power soccer championship winners of Adeline County are The Hot Wheels!"

Then he presented the team with a huge trophy that was four feet tall. It had a person in a wheelchair holding a soccer ball up in the air, and it was in gold. Under the gold person was a plaque that said:

The Hot Wheels
Adelina County's
First Power Soccer Team Champions
August 31, 2017

As the audience was cheering and celebrating, a reporter from VCSH went up to Tatianna and the champions, congratulating them and asking "What motivated you to have this big game televised?"

The reporter held the mic while Tatianna enthusiastically answered, "This team worked so hard at a sport that they love. Having so many people come watch and getting it televised is awesome. Plus, it helps raise awareness about power soccer and disabilities. I know there are people who think that being in a wheelchair or having a disability means you can't do what other people can do. Well, I hope from watching this game it will help those people realize that anything is possible. You can accomplish whatever you want if you put your mind to it. Right guys?" as Tatianna looked at her team.

The reporter found Justin in the crowd. "Congratulations on scoring the winning goal Justin! How did it feel? How long have you been playing power soccer?" the reporter asked.

Justin answered, "I've been playing power soccer for over a year. It feels awesome to be the one to score the winning goal!"

"I'm sure it does," replied the reporter. "Is there anything else you want to say to your new fans who are watching you on TV right now?"

"Yes! From being in a wheelchair, I've learned

that anything is possible if you put your mind to it. I also want to be the David Beckham for the power soccer communities."

"So, I take it that you're a big fan of David Beckham?"

Justin answered, "Yes! I hope to meet him one day!"

The reporter looked back at the camera and said, "David Beckham, if you're watching, you must come meet Justin and the rest of these kids! They are incredible! Reporting live from the Calistoga Arena in Adelina County. Once again, I want to congratulate The Hot Wheels for becoming the first power soccer champions!"

Conclusion

For Justin, this championship helped him find his spirit. Initially depressed, lonely, and in denial because of his accident, he learned how to adapt, communicate and get along with his newfound peers of disabled individuals.

Through the love and support of his family, his new friends, supporters, and mentors who encouraged and believed in him, he reconnected with his love for soccer, and brought his passion for the sport to a whole new level.

It was a long journey, but he became confident, embraced his new self, and most importantly he became a whole spirit.

Through becoming a power soccer champion, Justin found his destiny.

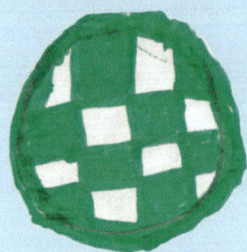

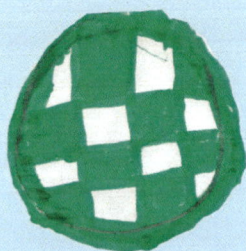

Other Books by Vanessa Castro

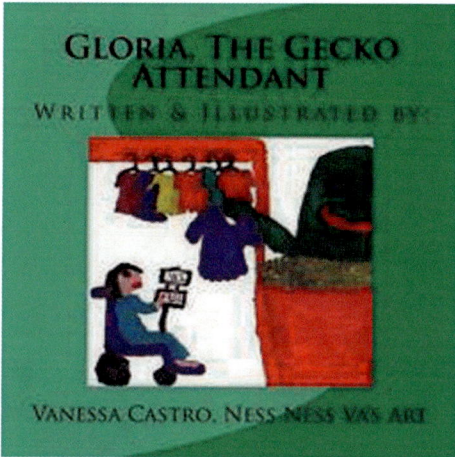

Gloria, the Gecko Attendant- A childrens' book (Ages 6-10) about a girl-named Sabrina in a wheelchair and her adventures with Gloria the Gecko, an unlikely helper.

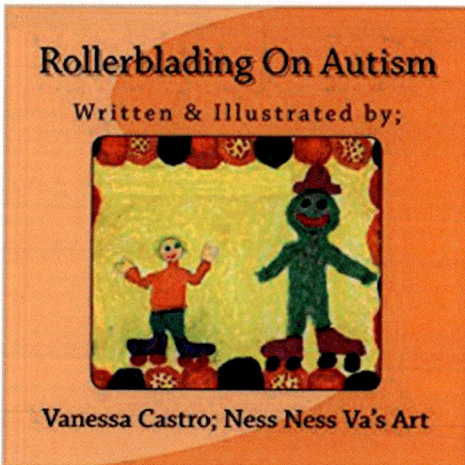

Rollerblading On Autism- A childrens' book (Ages 6-10) about boy named Kyle with Austism and his struggles and successes in friendship.

Visit nessnessva.com or amazon.com to purchase these books and learn more about Vanessa!

Made in the USA
Monee, IL
30 March 2024